I0158432

PASS PORT

ALSO BY AMY EVANS BAUER

Collecting Shells (Oystercatcher Press, 2011)
VierSomes 1: Rebecca Cremin, Amy Evans, Nat Raha, Frances Kruk
        (Veer Books, 2012)
The Sea Quells (Shearsman Books, 2013)
CONT. (Shearsman Books, 2015)
Stalking Gerard Manley Hopkins (Salient Seedling Press/
        Woodland Pattern Book Center broadside, 2016)
The Report of the Iraq Enquiry: Poetic Summary (The Larynx Press,
        ff imprint, 2017)
anti-fa-la-la: songs against statues 1. of posies (Tender Buttons Press/
        Face Press, Nectar Feed broadside, 2018)

First published in the United Kingdom in 2018 by
Shearsman Books
50 Westons Hill Drive
Emersons Green
BRISTOL
BS16 7DF

www.shearsman.com

Shearsman Books Ltd Registered Office
30–31 St. James Place, Mangotsfield, Bristol BS16 9JB
(this address not for correspondence)

ISBN 978-1-84861-622-6

Cover: *Lambis lambis* (Spider conch),
digital image, copyright © David Rees, 2018

AUDIO
Listen on the *Performance Research* YouTube Channel,
On Sea/At Sea special issue 21.2 (25 April 2016):
https://www.youtube.com/watch?v=z_h4VHm57qY

AMY EVANS BAUER

PASS PORT

SOUND((ING))S 1

SHEARSMAN BOOKS

PASS PORT

leagues   as
      under

I only   k no w   what

the waves'   economy of crash
after crash   sells me

s old me   already   long(ing) a go

second{s} h {and}   : holds

me kneelling

      no Life   in my
s old   Jacket

of h arms

        and the waving
          and dr owning

                I s [t]ing

forced by hate   to the co[a]st

               & long labour s

       could [not] forget the war

       And then would not go to the shhhip

becoming a(p)parent:

    b(u)oys scream
    in too deep

    can only Fother
    patch up, seal

                have forgotten
                Grand-mère

                left the children
                desolate of all kin ship

                SAVE adoption

s till—

depth

can be

he(a)rd

to canvas opinion

"*Traversier*
and *versier*"   said All,
                        Aboard

d own
she
went

Take 2:   soundings
but still   no L***
                &

s hound ing   the line

sound   ing   OUT

no benefits   at the INN

for   gotten
fore   cast

.   *a prediction*
               or estimate

               of future events, esp. coming weather
               or a financial tr end

                                          :

climate	[*of*]	fear
all	will	madden
commit ted	to	asylum
		seeking

we must[er],   ~~cannot~~
cheat   the ferry
men

see k
the c rest

H over   C raft

Rydeing

to Ports'   m*out*h

                 B fore

                 D over   to/and   D over

we   pass port
only   words in our pockets

terminal /ly
terminé

d Ova   &   d Ova

en   *core*

take ir   regular cycle

ultra *[an extremist]* sonic

               above the upper limit

               of human hearing

sonar maps berth—

finds skulls
among fish
scales waiting

for NET's GROWTH

cast ing c all:

sire ns   in
emerge   nce sea

prefer   perfect pitch
black

Ship's   c logged —

Triton   calculates
un/   conch
us   that
he   guesses
          at his   summms

will not   search
will not   res cue

Operation:

Triton's chest g rows
d ark   f ills
goes bust   as it

ge   states,
created   *to control*
borders   *not*
             to rescue

at sea

chart   our movement
by   Euro
stars   in the
    dark

longest   tunnel
    under

    smallest   of the shallow
    seas

&

P   [T]   O

IN THE   UN/LIKELY

EVE NT   OF A POETRY

S   *et*   O   and S

for   their   speed

of   t ravel

f/ache   their   story

and   flee,   take [all]   notes

CAP(s)

SIZE

Font s   *a receptacle for water*

tell s your fortune   for a fee:

no   papers

               s ailing

to   the

             DOC.

We must ~~(er r)~~:   do this by h *and*

in TenT ion   to find
shellter,   meats

b order   is t   b order

rapid   s hell

f   ire

well	come	aboard
in	come	abroad

LET	them
dr	OWN
LET	them
eat	sh**

cross   and a cross

crosser   than/then a crucifix

x   23 a day

head   ing for
sure

under   [over]
weigh   t:

S curvier and   S curvier
2 h ourglasses   at a time s

striking   bell e
watch(ed)   on and off

S W ooner

&

S W ooner

grass's   leave s

*shh*aped   like a heart

[,]   s *ave*

               u s

www.ingramcontent.com/pod-product-compliance
Lightning Source LLC
Chambersburg PA
CBHW021945040426
42448CB00008B/1254